To the reader:

Welcome to the DK ELT Graded Readers! These readers are different. They explore aspects of the world around us: its history, geography, science … and a lot of other things. They show the different ways in which people live now, and lived in the past.

These DK ELT Graded Readers give you material for reading for information, and reading for pleasure. You are using your English to do something real. The illustrations will help you understand the text, and also help bring the Reader to life. There is a glossary to help you understand the special words for this topic. Listen to the cassette or CD as well, and you can really enter the world of the Olympic Games, the *Titanic*, or the Trojan War … and a lot more. Choose the topics that interest you, improve your English, and learn something … all at the same time.

Enjoy the series!

To the teacher:

This series provides varied reading practice at five levels of language difficulty, from elementary to FCE level:

BEGINNER
ELEMENTARY A
ELEMENTARY B
INTERMEDIATE
UPPER INTERMEDIATE

The language syllabus has been designed to suit the factual nature of the series, and includes a wider vocabulary range than is usual with ELT readers: language linked with the specific theme of each book is included and glossed. The language scheme, and ideas for exploiting the material (including the recorded material) both in and out of class are contained in the Teacher's Resource Book.

We hope you and your students enjoy using this series.

Dorling **DK** Kindersley

LONDON, NEW YORK, SYDNEY, DELHI,
PARIS, MUNICH & JOHANNESBURG

Originally published as Eyewitness Reader
Winking, Blinking, Wiggling, and Waggling
in 2000, text © Brian Moses, and
adapted as an ELT Graded Reader for
Dorling Kindersley by

studio **cactus** ©

13 SOUTHGATE STREET WINCHESTER HAMPSHIRE SO23 9DZ

Published in Great Britain by
Dorling Kindersley Limited
9 Henrietta Street, London WC2E 8PS

2 4 6 8 10 9 7 5 3 1

Copyright © 2000
Dorling Kindersley Limited, London

A CIP catalogue record for this book is
available from the British Library.

ISBN 0-7513-2920-7

Colour reproduction by Colourscan, Singapore
Printed and bound in China by
L. Rex Printing Co., Ltd
Text film output by Mick Hodson Associates, UK

The publisher would like to thank the following
for their kind permission to reproduce their photographs:
c=centre; t=top; b=below; l=left; r=right

Ardea London Ltd: Kenneth W. Fink 10 br, 26 br, M. Watson 32
br; **Biofotos**: C. Andrew Henley 11 tr; **Bruce Coleman Collection
Ltd**: Alain Compost 13 b, Chrisler Fredriksson 31 b, Johnny
Johnson 25 br, Kim Taylor 32 cr; **Sylvia Cordaiy Photo Library
Ltd**: Colin Hoskins 18–19 b; **Julian Cotton Photo Library**: front
cover br; **Oxford Scientific Films**: David Cayless 27 t, Tim Jackson
18 tl, Steve Littlewood 16 c, Frank Schneidermeyer 23 br, Ian West
15 br; **Premaphotos Wildlife**: Ken Preston-Mafham 10 acl; **Tony
Stone Images**: front cover background; ©**Jerry Young**: 30 c.

Additional credits:
Peter Anderson, Geoff Brightling, Jane Burton, Geoff Dann, Mike
Dunning, Neil Fletcher, Steve Gorton, Frank Greenaway, Dave
King, Cyril Laubscher, Will Long and Richard Davies – Oxford
Scientific Films, Tracy Morgan, Kim Taylor and Jerry Young
(additional photography for DK); Lynn Bresler (for the index).

See our complete catalogue at

www.dk.com

ELT Graded Readers

ELEMENTARY A

ANIMALS LOOK!

Written by Caroline Laidlaw

Series Editor Susan Holden

A Dorling Kindersley Book

There are many different kinds of animal eyes and ears. This is an obvious fact and we can see some of the differences on these pages. For example, let's think about the position of the eyes. The cat and the fox have eyes at the front of their faces.

The caiman's eyes are high on top of its head.
What is the reason for these different positions?
What about ears? Let's think about shape,
as well as position. How are
they different in these
four animals?

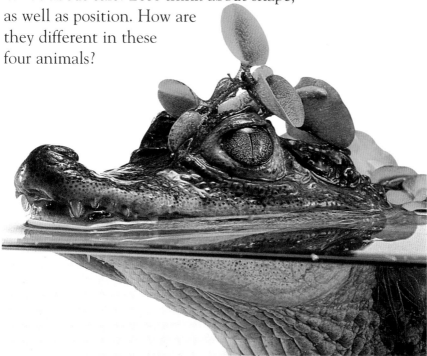

The cat and fox have quite large ears, facing forwards. They
are triangular, and they can move around. But where are the
eagle's and caiman's ears? In fact, do they
have any ears at all?
The answer is yes.
They have ears, but you
can't see them. Why are
these animals' ears so
different? The answer is
connected with evolution.
Through many thousands of
years, each animal slowly changed.

Our investigations begin with three predators (*hunters*) and one herbivore (*plant-eater*). Can you guess the names of these animals? The three hunters are active in dark places. In other words, where there is very little light.

This is a close-up of an owl's eye. It is very big because owls are active at night. Even in the poorest light their eyes are very sensitive. Human eyes need much stronger light than owls' eyes. And even then, we can only just see things in the dark.

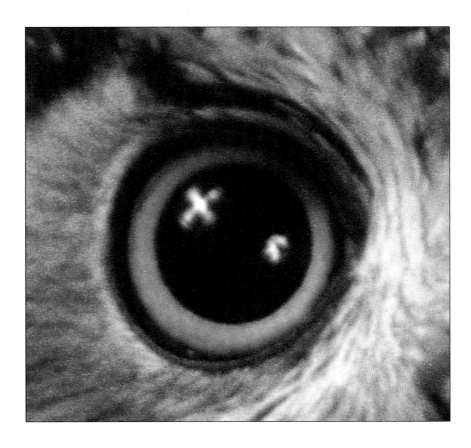

The squid lives in the sea. It has two large eyes, one on each side of its head. Like the owl, it needs large eyes because it hunts in the dark. It is an amazing fact that in structure the squid's eyes are almost the same as human eyes.

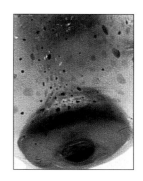

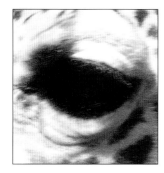

Which animal does this eye belong to? It's a giraffe's eye. This animal is active during the day. It has excellent eyesight. It can see a hungry lion or tiger from a great distance. And because it can run as fast as 56 kilometres an hour, it can usually escape its predators.

Here is the eye of a cat, another hunter. Cats usually hunt at night but sometimes they are active during the day, too. Their eyes work well in bright light or in very little light. Inside the eye, there is an extra layer of cells. They form a kind of mirror that reflects light and improves the image. Shine a flashlight at a cat, and its eyes glow like strange lights. (See "Eyes with mirrors" on page 9.)

As you can see, the owl's eyes are at the front of its head. This frontal position increases the angle of binocular vision. Both eyes together see the same object. With good binocular vision, the owl can judge distance accurately. It watches from a high place and keeps its prey in view.

There is something else about the owl's eyes: it cannot rotate them. Human eyes can move from side to side and up and down. But an owl cannot do this. In fact, the fixed eyes are useful because they can detect movement very well. And the owl's head can turn easily. An owl can see a moving mouse from a great distance.

The squid has ten tentacles (*arms*), not eight like an octopus. And squids are much more active than octopuses. There are many different kinds of squid, ranging from a few centimetres to around 18 metres.

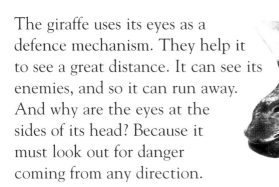

The giraffe uses its eyes as a defence mechanism. They help it to see a great distance. It can see its enemies, and so it can run away. And why are the eyes at the sides of its head? Because it must look out for danger coming from any direction.

The cat's eyes are at the front of the face, like the owl's eyes. And the cat also hunts at night. It can see in the dark about six times better than human beings.

Eyes with mirrors
Cats have a special mechanism at the back of their eyes. This acts like a mirror, and reflects light. This is very useful at night.

Spiders have four pairs of legs. Most spiders have eight eyes, like this jumping spider. The two biggest eyes are at the front, and the other eyes are all around the head. Other kinds of spiders may have six, four, or two eyes. Spiders that live in caves and dark places may not have any eyes at all.

These soft-bodied creatures do not have ears, but they have many special vibration receptors (*hairs*) on their bodies. These receptors can "hear" sounds from other spiders or sounds from their prey. They catch and eat mainly insects.

Spiders can communicate with each other. They make drumming noises with parts of their bodies. They can also communicate with special chemicals or pheromones. Male spiders can find females by following the scent in the silk web. But male spiders have a problem.

Very often a female wants to eat a male. He must send the right kind of vibrations through her web. Then the female knows that it is her mate on the web and not the next meal. But even careful males sometimes end up as food for the hungry female.

Four eyes
This little fish has very good visual equipment. It can spend a lot of time on the surface of the water, because it has unusual eyes. In fact, it has two eyes for looking up, and two for looking down.

The horsefly is an insect. Unlike a spider, the horsefly has three pairs of legs, and it has three parts to its body. It has two very big eyes on top of its head. We call these eyes compound eyes. Each compound eye has hundreds of tiny, individual lenses. And each tiny "eye" can see a bit of the whole picture. Some insects, particularly the hunters, can have as many as 30,000 "eyes". With so many tiny parts in their eyes, insects like this fly can see in almost every direction. This is why it is very difficult to catch a fly. It can always see you first!

Insects and human beings probably don't see colours in the same way. Insects can see ultra-violet light. This ability helps them to find nectar (*food*) in plants. They can see the ultra-violet guidelines that lead to the flower's nectar.

Vultures are a common sight in many parts of the world, such as Asia and Africa. They are birds of prey and must hunt for their food.

The vultures of Africa depend on thermals for successful hunting. A thermal is a rising column of hot air. Every morning, vultures sit in thorn trees and wait for the sun to rise and heat the land. Then a thermal begins to form. It catches beneath the vultures' wings and lifts the birds into the sky. Round and round they go, rising up the column of hot air. On top of the thermal, the vultures are hundreds of metres above the savannah. Here they can look down and, with their excellent eyesight, they can see a very long way. They look for dead or sick animals.

You can see that this vulture has very few feathers on its head and neck. This is necessary because vultures eat dead animals. They must keep their necks and heads as clean as possible at feeding time.

Tarsiers are very small animals. Even the largest kind of tarsier is only 15 centimetres long. They like to sit in trees and can hold on with special discs on their fingers and toes. They are carnivores and eat insects, frogs, lizards and small birds. But because they are night hunters, they need enormous eyes. They can see their prey in poor light, but they can also see any dangers. They can turn their heads in a complete circle. This is a very useful ability for such a small animal. It can easily see a predator that is looking for a tasty meal.

Moles spend nearly all their lives underground. They are only small, but they are very strong. They have very powerful front legs with five fingers on each hand. These can dig long tunnels in the ground. Most of the tunnels are like underground highways. But some of the tunnels are feeding stations. Here moles stop to eat worms or small insects. Or, sometimes, they use their feeding stations as larders for storing food.

When moles make tunnels, they make molehills at the same time, like the one below. Molehills are often a big problem for people with gardens. One mole can make as many as a hundred molehills.

Because moles live underground, they have very poor eyesight. Luckily, they have a highly developed sense of smell and touch. Their sensitive noses can smell and feel worms and insects in the ground. Moles are very hungry little animals. In one day they can eat at least half their body weight in food.

Earthworms are the favourite food of moles. These animals also live underground. But they have no eyes at all. In fact, earthworms do not have any specialised sense organs. But their skin is sensitive to light, and they can detect movement nearby.

They have short bristles (*hairs*) under their bodies. With the help of these hairs, the worms can move more easily through the ground.

Earthworms are important animals for agriculture. Huge numbers of worms live under the ground. They improve the soil in several ways. They pull dead leaves into the ground, and they also eat soil. The soil passes through their bodies and comes out in the form of wormcasts. This activity brings mineral-rich soil nearer the surface and is very good for growing plants.

Food stores for later
Moles catch a lot of worms. They bite off their heads and store them. A scientist once found a mole's store with more than 1,000 earthworms inside, in neat piles. The worms in the store do not die. But without their heads, they cannot escape. So the food is fresh.

This snail is a herbivore, like most other land snails. It usually eats dead leaves. It has got hundreds of tiny teeth on its radula *(tongue)*. Because the snail is always eating and chewing, the radula continually grows new teeth.

The snail's eyes are on the ends of two tentacles. Because it can move its tentacles around, it can get a good view of everything on the ground. It can also pull the tentacles into its head to protect its eyes. It can even pull its whole body into the hard shell. This is how the snail protects its soft body from danger, or from very cold or hot weather.

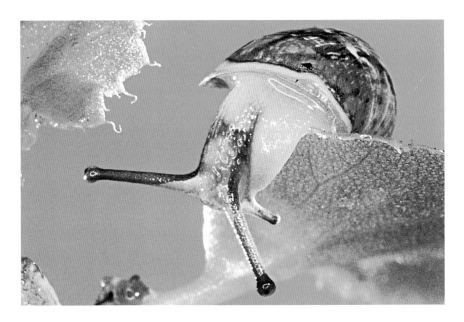

Snails do not have ears. They are silent animals. They can't hear, or communicate with sound. But they leave behind a silver trail. This is a slimy substance from the snail's "foot" under its body. It helps the snail to move smoothly and silently along the ground.

An extra eyelid
Birds of prey, like this eagle, have an extra eyelid. This is a clear film of skin that protects the eye. Birds of prey fly great distances and at great heights. And they often fly in very dusty air. The extra eyelids keep their eyes clean and healthy.

A camel also has a special mechanism that protects its eyes. In the desert it is often windy, with a lot of sand in the air. So camels have two rows of eyelashes. These protect the eyes from sand and from the bright sun. The ears also contain hairs to keep the sand out.

Here is a pair of meerkats – male and female. They are watching out for danger. They belong to a community of meerkats that lives in southern Africa.

Cats are also very watchful animals. They must keep their ears and eyes clean at all times.

A cat's ears can move in the direction of a sound. And they have large ears to collect as much sound as possible.

Bats have even larger ears. This is because bats have very poor eyesight. They hunt at night, and in the daytime they live in dark places, like caves. Their survival depends on their sense of hearing. You will read more about this later.

Elephants are the largest land animals in the world. Almost everything about an elephant is large, especially its head and ears. But an elephant's eyes are quite small in comparison with the rest of its body.

Do you recognise the ears on these pages? Which animals do they belong to? Here are some clues.

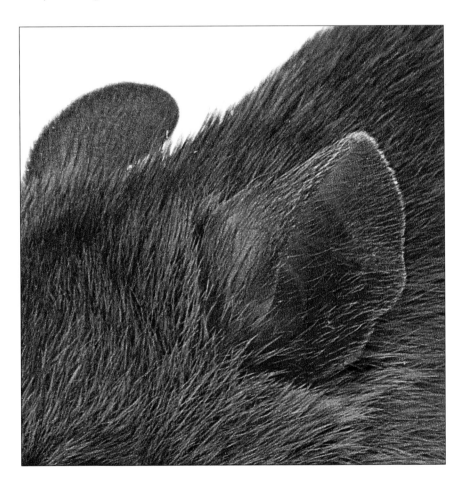

This is a very small animal. It has brown hair, a long tail, and tiny feet. It has large eyes and ears. It eats vegetarian food like seeds. This animal looks for food at night. But it must watch out, because it is the favourite food of many night hunters, like cats and owls.

This animal's ears are long and very sensitive. It lives in a burrow (*nest*) underground. In many countries children keep these animals as pets. But they are often a big problem for farmers. This is because they eat many kinds of green crops. In Australia, scientists tried to kill them with a disease.

Do you recognise these ears? No, they don't belong to a cat. They belong to a small animal that lives in the African bush. It is a good acrobat and can jump from tree to tree. Its body is only twenty centimetres long but it can jump up to five metres.

These ears belong to a dangerous carnivore. It is orange and black and hunts at night. A hundred years ago, there were many of these animals in the world. But now they are endangered, and very few of them are left. In the past, people hunted them for their beautiful striped skin.

Now turn the page, and find out the names of these animals.

Mice, like many other animals, can hear much better than human beings. Young mice in danger can make ultrasonic sounds that the human ear cannot detect. The mother mouse can hear these sounds from a distance. Then she hurries back to protect her babies.

Mice, rabbits and other animals have long sensitive hairs on their faces. They are very useful because these animals find their way with them.

A rabbit's large eyes are in a high position at the side of the head. They can see clearly in poor light, and at night. The position of the eyes gives good vision in every direction.

Rabbits and mice often hunt for food at night. The cooler, humid night air carries scents better than dry air in daylight. This is why night hunters usually have very sensitive noses.

This is a bushbaby and not a cat. But it is a bit like a cat, with large eyes at the front of its face. It has good binocular vision, so it can judge distance well. This is important for hunters and for animals that jump from branch to branch in the night. The bushbaby's large ears can detect the sounds of insects, its food.

Tigers are members of the cat family. They are also night hunters. They have very sensitive ears, excellent eyesight and a very good sense of smell. They can hear small animals in the grass. But other animals usually don't hear tigers because these huge cats move so carefully and silently. They can stand still for a long time, but are always ready to run.

White spots
Tigers have white spots on the backs of their ears. Perhaps tiger cubs (*young tigers*) can see the white spots on their mother's ears. They see the spots and follow them. It is a good way to stay close to their mother.

Dogs have a highly developed sense of hearing. Their ears are much more sensitive than human ears. They can hear ultrasonic sounds from small animals like mice. And they can hear the high sound of whistling – something the human ear can't hear. And because dogs are so intelligent, they can use their sense of hearing to help people in many ways. This, for example, is a sheepdog. The shepherd whistles and sends the dog instructions from a distance. The dog understands the meaning of the whistling and follows the instructions. Dogs have good eyesight too. With eyes at the front of their faces, they have good binocular vision.

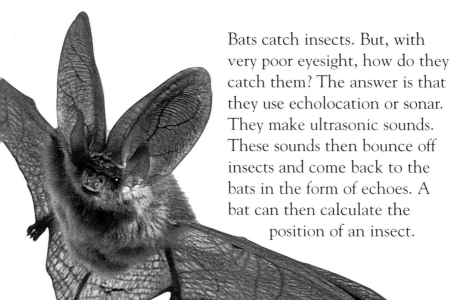

Bats catch insects. But, with very poor eyesight, how do they catch them? The answer is that they use echolocation or sonar. They make ultrasonic sounds. These sounds then bounce off insects and come back to the bats in the form of echoes. A bat can then calculate the position of an insect.

So its ears are very important indeed. This is why they are so big.

Bats sleep during the day in dark places such as caves. They hang upside down by their feet. And they live together in large groups. Bats can fly, but they are nothing like birds. A bat's wing consists of a thin layer of skin that stretches across four long fingers. And there is a little thumb at the front with a claw on it. The wing skin also stretches down to the legs and tail.

Whales communicate
Sound travels very well through water. And whales make good use of this. They don't have visible ears, but their inner ears are very good. They can communicate across enormous distances. Scientists believe that whale songs travel hundreds of kilometres.

There are several kinds of foxes in the world, but the red fox is the most common. Its habitat ranges from the far north of North America, Europe, and Asia, to the deserts of Central America and North Africa. Perhaps they are successful because they can eat almost any kind of food.

They eat small animals, birds, eggs, and worms. But they also eat fruit and berries.

Foxes can hear the smallest sound with their sensitive ears. And they have very good eyesight as well. What can you tell from the position of the eyes on the fox's head? Do they have good binocular vision? The answer is yes. This is because they are mainly carnivores, and hunt for food.

An excellent sense of hearing
A fox can even hear a worm moving in the grass. The worm makes a quiet noise with its bristles as it moves. In no time at all, the fox finds the worm and eats it.

The rhinoceros has poor eyesight. It cannot see things clearly at a distance. But it has a good sense of smell, and good hearing too. It can turn its large ears to pick up sounds in the distance.

Kangaroos can rotate their ears as well. They can find the exact direction of a sound. But during the day they are not very active. They usually sleep under the shade of a tree. At night, however, kangaroos must use all their senses. They have large eyes that help them see in poor light. And their sensitive noses lead them to the sweetest grasses and plants. But, most important of all, they must listen for predators.

Not all animals have ears on the outside of their bodies. Many have inner ears, but no visible outer ears. Whales and birds, for example, have a good sense of hearing, but no outer ears. Birds' ears are two small holes in the sides of their heads. You can't see the ears because feathers cover them.

It is an advantage to have an ear on each side of the head. The animal can locate the source of a sound very quickly. The brain instinctively calculates the time difference between the arrival of the sound at each ear. It is only an infinitesimal time, but enough to locate the source of a sound. This is why the alarm call of many birds is one continuous sound. A predator, such as an eagle, cannot locate this kind of sound quickly. A series of short sounds is much easier to locate.

A bird's ears also control its balance. This is also true for many other animals, including human beings.

Fish have only inner ears. Their sense of hearing is generally good. People who keep carp sometimes ring a bell before feeding time. The fish hear the bell and come for their food.

Snakes depend on their senses of smell, taste, and touch. Many snakes have poor eyesight. And their hearing is poor as well. In fact, snakes don't have outer ears. But they can pick up vibrations that travel through the ground. From these vibrations, they can detect movement nearby. They know the direction an animal is coming from. The vibrations also tell the snake about the size of the animal.

Snakes have a specialised sense of smell. They can taste and smell things with their tongues. A few snakes also have special heat sensors that detect heat from the bodies of animals. This helps them find and kill prey in total darkness.

Frog ears and eyes
Frogs hunt mainly by sight. Their large eyes can see well in daylight and at night. Frogs have a large, flat layer of skin behind their eyes. This is called an eardrum. They need good hearing because they have many enemies.

The fennec is the smallest of all the foxes. The head and body measure about 38 centimetres, and the ears about 15 centimetres. But why does it have such big ears? One clue is its habitat, the deserts of northern Africa and Saudi Arabia. In the hottest hours of the day, the ears cool the fox's blood.

Blood flows through the thin layer of skin in the ears. Air blows over the ears and cools the blood. This is a clever adaptation to habitat. Even more amazing is the fact that the fennec never drinks. It gets all the water it needs from its food.

Big ears can also pick up more sound. This is a good thing for the fennec fox, because there is very little to eat in the desert habitat. Especially the kind of food this carnivore enjoys – small animals, such as lizards and insects.

Each of an African elephant's ears can be 1.7 metres across. The big ears on an elephant have the same function as the fennec's ears. They cool the elephant's blood on very hot days. As with the fox, the air blows over the ears and the blood cools down.

Elephants, especially the bulls (*males*), sometimes use their huge ears in another way. They hold their ears out and flap them. They want to look bigger than they really are. This behaviour usually happens during the mating season. But elephants will hold out their ears at other times as well. It is a warning to enemies that they are very strong, powerful animals.

Most of the time, however, elephants are gentle animals. They communicate with each other in many ways and with all their senses. The position of ears and trunks can show their mood, such as fear, anger, or contentment.

Glossary

binocular vision
Both eyes seeing the same object.

bristle
A thick, short hair.

carnivore
A meat-eating animal.

compound eye
The eye of an insect, with many individual parts.

defence mechanism
Something that an animal uses to protect itself.

echolocation
Sounds which bounce off objects and help to locate them.

endangered species
A species that is rare, and that might become extinct.

evolution
The gradual change and development of plants and animals over many thousands of years.

eyelashes
Small hairs that grow along the edge of each eyelid.

eyelid
The piece of skin that moves to cover the eye.

herbivore
A plant-eating animal.

lens
A piece of transparent material that focuses light.

molehill
A small heap of earth thrown up from a mole's tunnel.

mood
A feeling such as happiness, anger, fear.

native animal
An animal species that belongs to a particular country or habitat.

nectar
The sweet liquid collected by insects (and sometimes birds) from flowers.

pheromone
A chemical produced by an animal to communicate with another animal of the same species.

predator
An animal that kills and eats other animals.

prey
Animals that are killed and eaten by other animals.

radula
The tongue of a snail.

sonar
Using sounds.

tentacle
A long, boneless arm used for feeling and holding.

ultra-violet light
Light which the human eye cannot see.

vegetarian food
Food that contains no meat.

wormcast
A tube-like pile of earth left on the surface of the ground by an earthworm.